Sand Beneath My Feet

Janet Doble

For my family

Contents

Introduction and Acknowledgements

Cornwall needs no introduction.   It is as popular today as it was when I was growing up in the 1960's and 70's, probably more so.

I began writing these poems in 2020 during the early stages of the COVID-19 pandemic. What began as a creative activity developed into a wish to return to my roots, to capture the love I have always felt for the county of my birth. I also hoped to express, poetically, a little of the history and culture of Cornwall, particularly around the coastal resort of Perranporth.

This book is for anyone, young or old, who has felt a connection with Cornwall.

With special thanks to Rachel Bingham for her illustrations.

Acknowledgements to Captain William Roberts for his book "Reminiscences of Perranporth from the year 1833" and Bill Trembath for "Perranporth and Perranzabuloe Parish". Both books helped clarify background details on mining and smuggling in the Perranporth area.

Janet Doble

Sand Beneath My Feet

Sand beneath my feet
  Evokes the memory
Of a Cornish childhood,
  Of summers by the sea.

Postcard perfect beach
  Of sands and rocks and seas,
Soon filled with stripy windbreaks
  And sounds of families.

The weather didn't matter,
  We had a beach hut there
To shelter from the rain and wind
  And sometimes sunshine's glare.

Saffron buns and stewed flask tea
  With gritty sand was laced.
Safe within our beach hut
  The wind around us raced.

Ever present sand
  That took on any form
From silk between my toes
  To stinging wind-whipped storm.

Or hardened by retreating sea
  The perfect castles made,
And tunnels, sculptures, roads and more,
  Built simply with a spade.

An ever-present backdrop,
  That's what it seems to me,
From childhood through to teen years.
  Golden memory.

Atlantic

I've always been in awe of you,
Your dazzling displays of power,
Slumberous sighs, resounding roars,
Or frothy surf around your shores.

When tranquillity I needed
You were always there,
Your sound a melody
Your presence soothing me.

Sometimes your face appeared so calm
When underneath there lurked
Turbulent currents, a dangerous tow
Pulling, dragging all below.

At other times I watched you rage,
Tumultuous tides and massive waves
Crashing against the steadfast cliffs,
Tearing rocks that smash to bits.

And how you've dazzled! Diamanté dressed,
Capturing the play of the sun,
Rippling light across the strait
To enchant, bewitch and captivate.

Sometimes the colour of tourmaline,
Mauve and turquoise, aquamarine,
Merging into indigo
Every hue of blue, grey, green,
Reflecting sky and depths unseen.

You bring such fun in summertime,
Swimming, surfing, paddling.
Playful waves that tickle my feet,
Laughter, shivers, what a treat!

Dear friend, I miss you when I'm gone.
Other seas just aren't the same.
I miss your depths, your subtlety.
In you I sense eternity.

In the Shallows

Here in the shallows
  The tide's in retreat,
Sucking the sand
  That's surrounding my feet.

I can see below,
  Through the sea's clarity,
There's a light-formed work
  Of supreme artistry.

On a canvas made from golden sand,
  Watery forms take shape.
Textures and patterns take hold, then dissolve,
  As the rays of the sun penetrate.

At times a mosaic of cracked golden light
  Is created by sun on the sea,
Ever changing with the shifting tide
  And the sand that ripples constantly.

A sudden shoal of tiny grey fish
  Cast shadows across the sea bed,
Briefly a part of this ocean montage,
  Edging close, then darting ahead.

And drifting close to the surface,
  Its tentacles hidden from view,
A jelly fish, striped in orange and brown,
  Adds shades of a different hue.

The light is changing; it's time to move on,
  Bid this watery art adieu.
Leave to the ocean its masterful skill,
  Creating displays ever new.

Cathedral Caverns - *Vugah-en-Plunder*

The tide was at full ebb.
Perhaps one of those days
When we could walk around the Point
And visit the great caves.

At the bidding of the tide,
It was a rarity
To enter this cathedral
Carved out by the sea.

I felt quite vulnerable
Walking on this sand,
Only present for a time -
It was really borrowed land,
Borrowed from the sea
Who owned this stretch of beach.
Don't spend too long exploring
If home you'd like to reach!

And high above my head,
The unforgiving cliffs
Remind me of the folly
Of doing things like this.

And yet it was so special
To enter this vast place,
Its yawning mouth, its dripping roof,
Its dark engulfing space.

A haven once for smugglers
Who came at dead of night,
Then hoisted up their booty
Through shafts away from sight.

Where did it lead?
I heard it said
It stretched far underground
Then ended ignominiously,
Within a car park bound.

The tide has turned,
Criss-crossing waves
Are lapping round our feet.
Time to bid farewell now
And beat our own retreat.

Mined Out

It's difficult to visualise
This place in former times.
A resort now steeped in tourism
That once relied on mines.

The field behind the village,
That's now a playing space,
With nearby grass-laid tennis courts,
Was once a hellish place.

Engine houses, tips and dumps,
Water wheels for power.
Machinery of every kind
Throbbing by the hour.

Copper was extracted
From breaking up the ore.
Fortunes could be made or lost,
But a miner's life was poor.

Underneath the village
Miles of galleries run,
Dug out by the miners
Who rarely saw the sun.

A miserable existence,
Working underground,
Long, hard days, a meagre wage,
To this their lives were bound.

Two copper mining companies ruled,
Neighbours filled with enmity.
Litigation brought by one
Sparked the end of industry.

What happened to the piles of waste?
There's nothing left to see.
It was used to build the road
That leads to Bolingey.

Look high up on the cliffs
If remains you want to see,
Mine shafts, waste and reddish scree,
Still scar the scenery.

Whilst down below
The golden sands
Tourists now entice.
Pasties, ice-creams, gifts galore
Make for a different life.

Suspicion

How came he by the money
To build those dwellings there?
Could he be the one
Who gave us such a scare?

Who played a treacherous game
Near gave us all away?
How came he by that money
On just a miner's pay?

Contraband they called it.
For us, 'twas normal trade,
Balancing high taxes,
An easier life it made.

Cherbourg was our ship to France
And many a run we'd made,
Unloading her with our small boats
And winched up through the cave,
On to mules, then hurried away
Free from the Customs' gaze.

That time we took him on,
That quiet moonlit night,
The Revenue men were watchful,
Their clippers out of sight.

We landed just one boat-load
And hid it all away,
Made good our own escape
Whilst *Cherbourg* lay at bay.

The wind got up, away she raced,
The clippers in her wake,
Needing to reach France
Not a moment could she waste.

She made it just in time,
Guns firing at her stern,
But that was her last run
- Sold, never to return.

Our smuggling days were over,
The risk was far too great.
If caught, we knew for certain
Botany Bay would be our fate.

It wasn't much long after
He came into some wealth.
How came he by that money?
Was it from some act of stealth?

How did he grow so rich?
I couldn't rightly say.
But I reckon it was him
That gave the game away!

The Lost Church

Deep within the dunes
There lies a sacred place;
Long ago a Saint's abode,
It remains a tranquil space.

The ancient oratory,
Once protected in a concrete shell,
Was vulnerable to flooding
And a pool outside would swell.

When young, I saw a lake of myths
And wondered what it held.
What mysteries lay around you?
What stories could you tell?

Stories of how long ago
An Irish Saint arrived,
Floated on a millstone
And washed up by the tide.

St Piran settled on this spot,
Perhaps once rich and green,
And built a simple oratory
A holy life to lead.

He established Christianity
Upon pagan Cornish land.
His oratory became a church
Until engulfed by sand.

It must have been a battle to
Keep sand and flood away,
Until it was too much.
Time came to move away.

On higher ground, another church
With a Celtic cross beside,
But that too was abandoned,
With sand on every side.

Walking here, these days, can seem
Quite bleak and bare of trees,
Windswept pathways through the dunes,
Coarse grass and distant seas.

But skylark song accompanies us
And tiny flowers create
A carpet thrown across our path
With patterns intricate.

Perhaps we're not quite pilgrims
But we have reverence nonetheless.
This ancient Cornish holy place
Connects us to deep sacredness.

To the Beach

Do we have all we need for our day by the sea?
Beach towels and costumes
And a good book for me.
We'll enjoy a nice picnic and plenty to drink.
A flask might be useful
And deckchairs I think.

The breeze off the sea can often be strong.
A windbreak and mallet
We must bring along.
It sometimes turns cold at the end of the day.
Perhaps there's a fleece
I can just pack away.

Suncream and sunhats so we don't find ourselves burned.
It's best to be safe in the sun
I have learned.
Rubber soled sandals for scrambling around
On barnacled rocks
And rough cliffside ground.

The firm sand is perfect for beach games and cricket.
We can take bats and balls
And maybe a wicket.
The kids will be happy with bucket and spade
And flags to adorn
All the castles they've made.

If the sea is calm, we'll take kayak and oars
But if surf's up, we'll need
Wetsuits and boards.
We'd best have some money, as hiring is dear,
And we'll need some for ice creams
And maybe a beer.

It's only a day trip, but so much to take
And all of this planning
Can make my head ache.
I know we'll have fun, but I'm beginning to think
    We've everything here
    But the kitchen sink!

From Flat Rocks

Rough steps cut in the crumbly cliff
Lead from the sandy beach,
And dusty paths guide me through
To a grassy ledge and ocean view.

Busy beach noise muted now,
Filtered through the marram grass,
Whilst below, the ever-present sea
Murmurs its own melody.

Beyond the beach stretch headlands,
Outlined in hazy grey,
And waves that break around their base
Send plumes of smoking spray.

A single gannet out at sea,
Wings drawn back in arrow head.
A dive that's elegant and sleek
Plunging in the ocean's deep.

You've caught the attention of a gull,
His greedy eyes
Have spied your prize.
A chase ensues – he's after your catch.
Who will win? It's hard to tell,
He's lazy, but hungry as well.

Amidst the surfers on their boards
You swoop and swerve and twist and soar.
He's given up, all is done.
Away you fly with the fish you've won!

From the Tor

Settlements and farming,
Mining and tourists,
  All have left their mark
  On ancient West Penwith.

Yet something underlying
Continues to exist,
Draws me like a magnet,
Has power to bewitch.

A part of this wild landscape
And commanding higher ground,
This hill provides a perfect view
Of grandeur all around.

So many times I've been here,
Picnicked on this tor,
Climbed its rocky pancake stacks
That beckon to explore.

I've walked the winding track
To the Iron-Age hill fort,
Past the stunted oaks
And scrubby bristling gorse.

From here I see stretched out
The familiar, much-loved view
And still I catch my breath
At beauty ever-new.

On both sides lie the ocean
Reflecting the vast sky.
To the north extends a stretch of sand
Where a lighthouse marks the hidden land.

Due South, the hazy sky dissolves
Into the glimmering sea,
Where rising proud from this soft sheen
St Michael's Mount is plainly seen.

Beyond the tor are rugged hills
That range towards the West.
Years of farming can't disguise
The granite base on which they rest.

Granite everywhere is strewn
Upon this rough terrain,
Or here and there creating walls
Exposed to Cornish rain.

Up here, I sense deep in my soul
The elemental power
  Of nature: earth and sky and sea
  Expressed in its raw purity.

Of Loss and Gain

Gateway to another world
Past the cattle grid,
Over the field until I see
The estuary in front of me.

South west breeze, soft sweet air,
Hills that fold, and place
Both winding river and myself
In their gentle arms' embrace.

Absorbed within this scene
My mind begins to trace
Questions of another time,
Of those whose dwelling was this place.

    What was your story Thomas?
    Were you young when you came here?
    Did it then entrance you too
    And become so very dear?

    Did you long for Cornish rain to clear
    So you could race down to the shore
    And clamber over slippery rocks
    The better to explore?

    Did you watch in fascination
    The flashing silver light
    Of mullet in the shallows
    Flipping in delight?

    Did you skim stones with your siblings
    Or hide behind a tree?
    Climb the sessile oaks
    That reach towards the sea?

    Or watch the river traffic
    Laden with cargo?
    Plying wealth within the county,
    Unloading in Truro.

Could you have imagined
The river of today?
Its chugging little motorboats,
The massive ships at bay.

Perhaps you loved it dearly,
And when it was your own
You added grandeur to the house,
To create a gracious home.

Born to wealth from copper and tin,
For some a mining hell.
Your grandfather earned a pretty name:
"Guinea-a-minute" Daniell.

But fortunes can be won and lost
And this would be your fate.
You lacked the business acumen
To keep your money safe.

Your spending frittered all away,
Then metal prices fell.
There was no choice but to flee to France
The house and grounds to sell.

Almost two hundred years have passed
Since those turbulent days.
Could you have guessed the public now
Would wander your pathways?

Could you know that I would share
This tranquil loveliness?
And discover for myself the truth
That beauty simply is?

The Thief

"Outrage, horror,
Blatant attack!
He saw, he swooped,
He knocked off my hat!

My ice-cream! My sandwich!
My favourite meat pie!"
You'd better watch out
When a seagull flies by.

He's into the rubbish,
He's scrounging around,
The bins get upturned
And waste hits the ground.

He'll be hunting for more,
He's greedy for sure.
Oh, you'd better watch out
When a seagull's about.

But your home was elsewhere,
Not the bin, not the pie.
You ruled from the sky
Where your bright yellow eye
Spied fish in the sea
For your hungry family.

How have you fallen,
Once mighty sea gull!
From King of the Seas
To Thief of Pasties.

Home Again

The rooftop here is perfect
For perching way up high,
Giving me the ideal view
Of people walking by.

From here, I've learned to steal
Fresh morsels for my brood,
It's what I simply love to do –
Go out and find good food!

But I see from the mirror I've changed quite a bit,
More fat than before, and rather unfit,
More mean than lean,
An eating machine.
I don't like to see
This image of me!

Where was that place you spoke of before?
Of skies and seas and pristine white shore.
Perhaps I could go there
And give it a try.
I'll stretch out my wings
And fly there, just fly ....

What's that down below?
I'm sure it's a fish,
Still moving, not battered,
Not part of a dish.

I'll aim, I'll dive,
I'll catch it for sure.
That's tasty! That's perfect!
Like nothing before.

Oh look at me now!
I'm back home at last.
Lord of the skies
And ocean so vast.

Peppermint Tide

The beach is bathed in late summer sun,
And bright with families
Intent on having last-minute fun
Before Autumn's call to work's begun.

High tide; the sea is streaming fast,
Almost knocks me off my feet,
All froth and foam, it makes me laugh.
My clothes are wet, but what delight
To be standing here, this September day
Gazing out across the bay.

Today the sea is peppermint green,
Layer upon layer of fondant cream
Building up,
And pouring in,
Whilst chocolate coloured seaweed rocks
With surf are sometimes iced,
    As wave on wave of breaking sea
    Burst on the shore with energy.